Wisconsin REFLECTIONS

Photography by Darryl R. Beers

Haikus by Raymond Reed Hardy

Trails Books
BOULDER

Photography copyright © 2014 by Darryl R. Beers

Text copyright © 2014 by Raymond Reed Hardy

Original concept and design by Christine M. Schultz

All rights reserved. No part of this book may be reproduced in any form, except for brief reviews, without the written permission of the publisher.

Published by
Trails Books
a Big Earth Publishing company
3005 Center Green Drive, Suite 225
Boulder, CO 80301
800-258-5830
bigearthpublishing.com

Cover and text design: D.K. Luraas
Front cover photo: Loon Lake, Ashland County
Back cover photo: Rio Creek, Kewaunee County

ISBN: 978-1-934553-49-7

Library of Congress Control Number: 2013957494

Printed in China by Everbest Printing Co, Ltd through Four Colour Imports, Ltd.

Introduction
By Raymond Reed Hardy

The history of the haiku poetic form goes back more than 500 years with roots among Buddhist writers in both China and Japan. While the form has evolved during those years, it continues to be recognizable as a separate poetic genre. The common elements that define the genre are the traditional syllable format consisting of three lines of five, seven, and five syllables each, the emphasis on nature, and the "cut" or "twist" that highlights a shift in perspective that is often, though not always, present in haiku poems.

    The initial idea which led to my writing haikus inspired by Darryl's photographs arose during a conversation that Darryl and I shared as we made the three-hour journey to and from a Zen retreat in central Wisconsin in 2004. As Darryl shared his story I heard him say, "I have taken about 10,500 photographs of nature scenes around Wisconsin and Michigan." And he heard me say, "I love nature photos. Haikus are typically about nature. I wonder if I could use your photos as the inspirational seeds for some of my haikus." That retreat was the beginning of a slowly deepening friendship and collaborative work that—with the creative influence of Darryl's fiancée, Christine Schultz—has produced two books of paired pictures and poems with a third, focused specifically on Wisconsin trees, under development.

    The reader is encouraged to see in these photographic and poetic images both the beauty of the natural world and the playfulness of the human spirit, to giggle with sudden glee, or to feel the pinch of an appreciative tear. And throughout your journey through this book and any of our other books please remember, we did this work just for the fun of it. We still have about 10,350 slides to look at. There may be more fun on the way. Enjoy!

Nature's droplet lens

skewered on dwarf iris frond,

whole world inverted.

Dwarf Lake Iris, The Ridges Sanctuary, Door County

A lone seagull rests

seeking breakfast's telltale fins

revealed by dawn's light.

Pond Nets at Sunrise, Lake Michigan, Algoma

Peaceful hidden creek

dusted with fall maple leaves

beckons, come deeper.

Rio Creek, Black Ash Swamp, Kewaunee County

All this wondrous light

just reflections of the sun,

our beloved source.

Moonrise at Kewaunee South Pierhead Light, Lake Michigan, Kewaunee

Early autumn's warmth

adorns this simple harbor,

one man's paradise.

Little Birch Lake, Laona

Pink mist's reflection

holds still this placid shoreline

'tween thumb and fingers.

Bear Lake, Nicolet National Forest

Sun sits like a ghost,

its red heat glazing the bay

yielding to darkness.

Bay of Green Bay, from Communiversity Park, Green Bay

The eye settles here

drenched in perfect harmony

dancing light and cloud.

Sunset over Juddville Bay, Door County

Bright golden sunset

burnishes our warm lagoon.

Come on mom, let's swim!

Egg Harbor, Door County

Romance on the ice?

So easily imagined.

A sweet illusion.

Sturgeon Bay Ship Canal North Pierhead Light, Lake Michigan, Door County

Scallops above frame

a brilliant blue horizon.

It's sailboat heaven!

Eagle Harbor, Ephraim, Door County

Summer's sublime scene,

a thin grove of sailboat masts

safe in their harbor.

Fish Creek, Door County

The eye is confused

tight vertical symmetry,

reflection's magic.

East River, Green Bay

Palest reflection

smears delightful fall colors

above bending grass.

Lake Emily, Portage County

Lungs fill for great sigh.

It has a will of its own.

Inexpressible.

Devil's Lake, Devil's Lake State Park

Fleecy dark green hills

above marvelous wetland,

wind smeared reflections.

Mississippi River, Vernon County

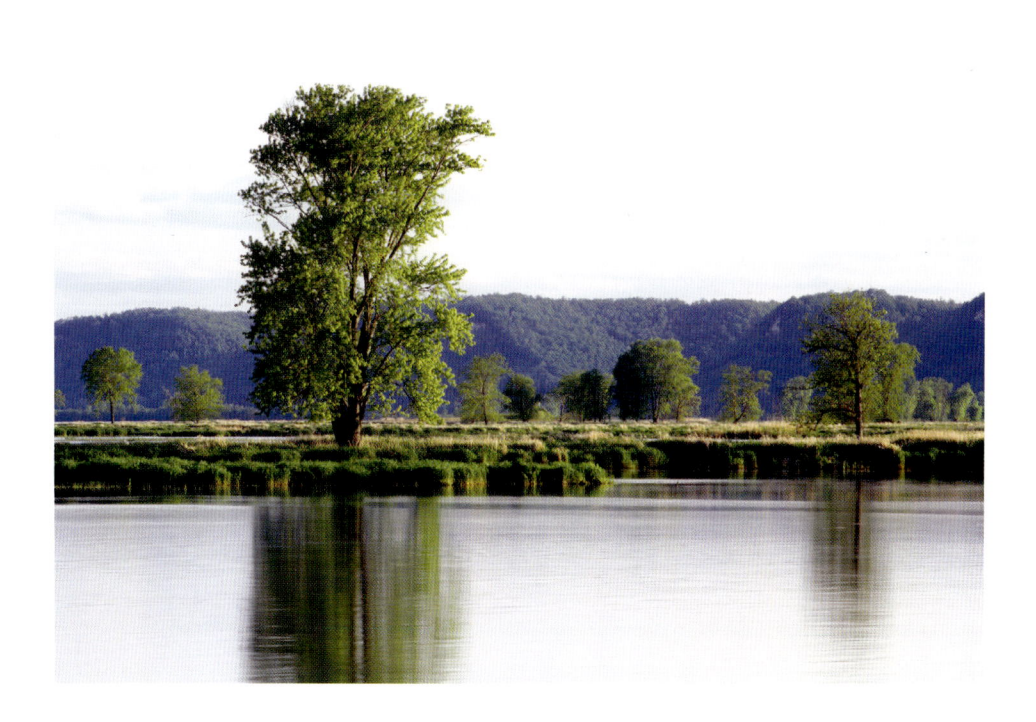

Dragonfly pauses

shining silver wings aglow,

orange spots delight.

Red Skimmer Dragonfly, Devil's Lake State Park

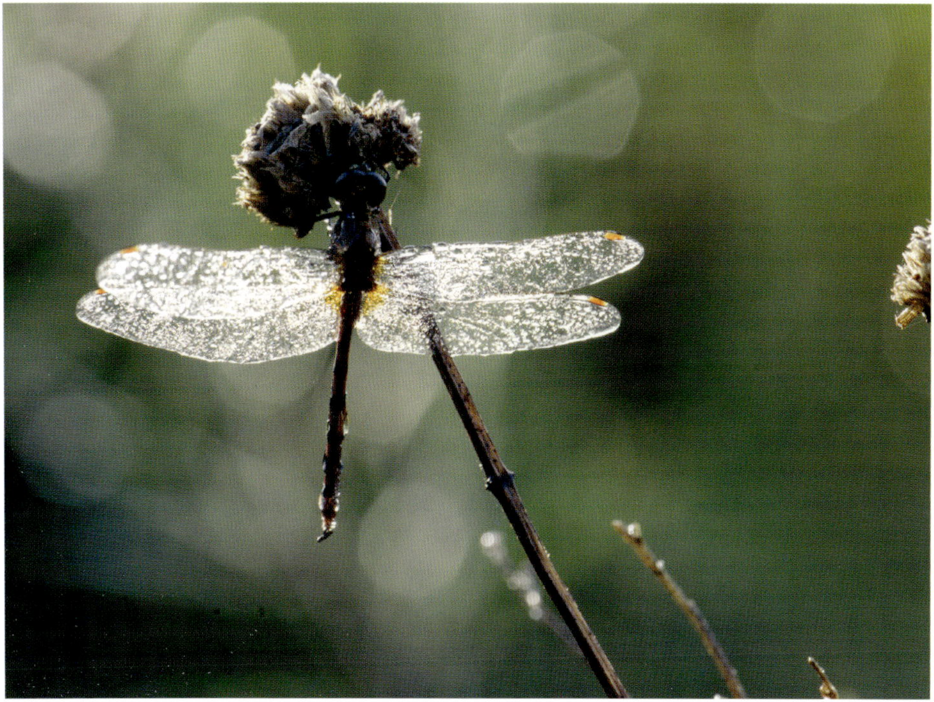

Clouds hide the true source.

Water claims the golden sheen,

but we know the truth.

Lake Superior at Sand Bay, Apostle Islands National Lakeshore

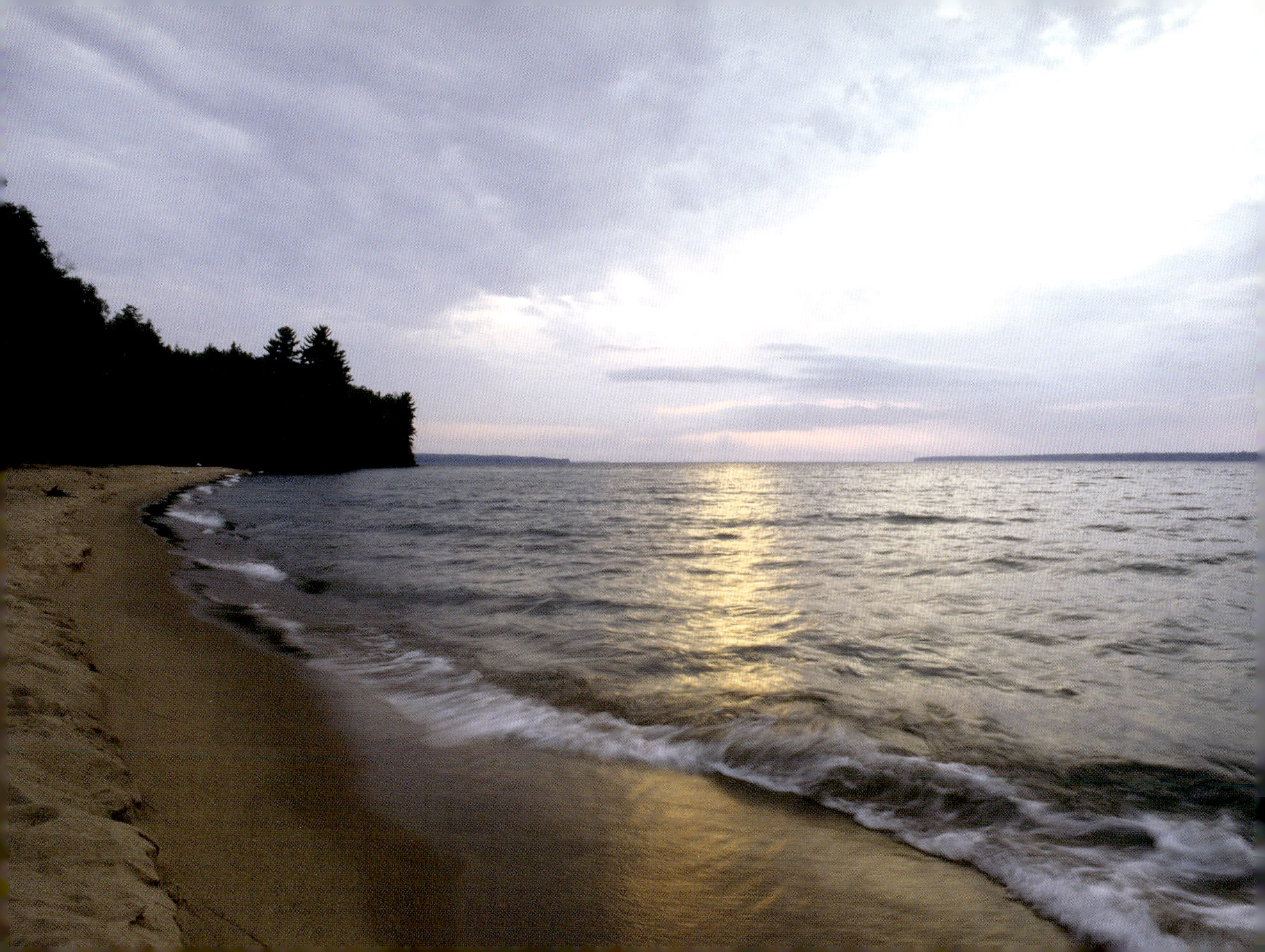

Nature reaches up,

tall masts, spiky poplar trees,

all worship water.

Fond du Lac Harbor, Lake Winnebago

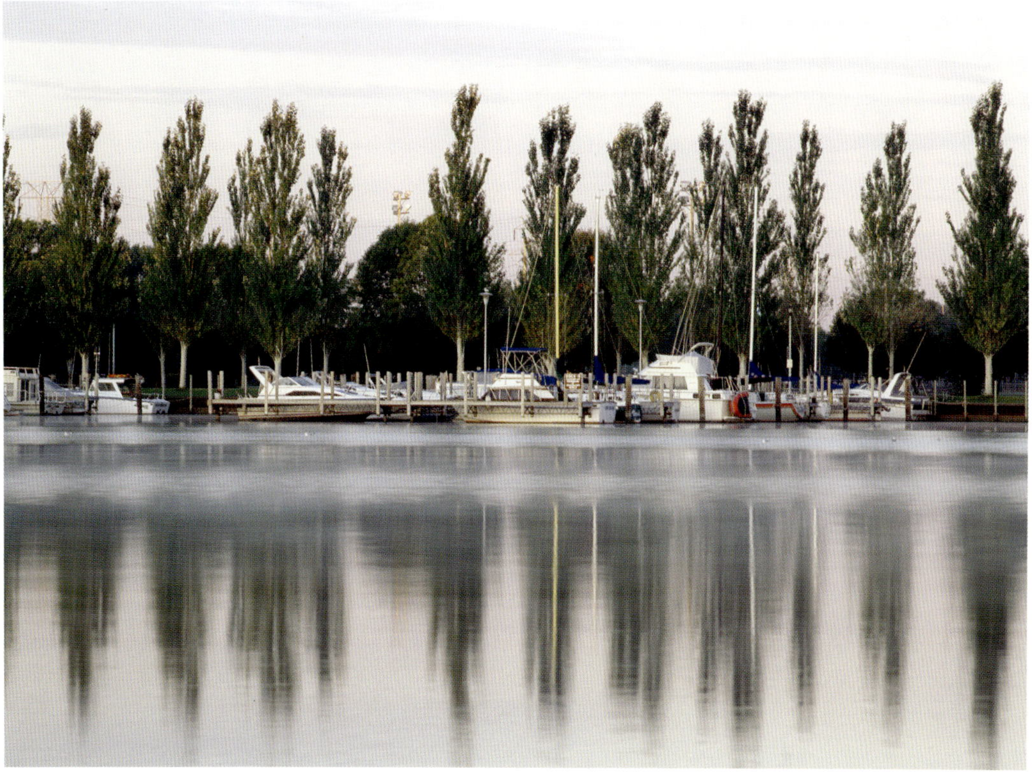

Dawn's buttery sun

greets this lowly speck—a ship—

sailing slowly home.

Freighter at Sunrise, Lake Superior, Bayfield

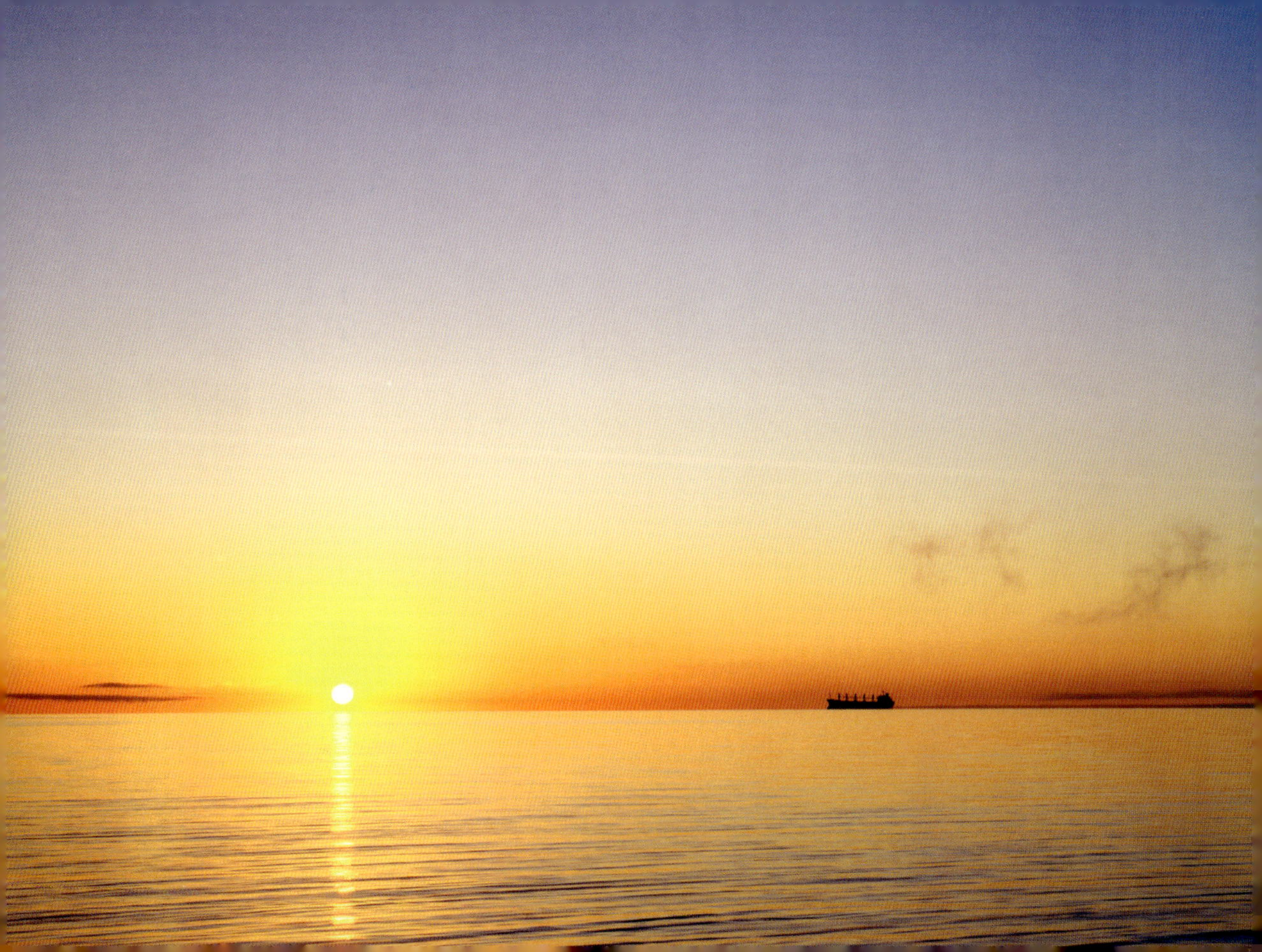

Slow, lazy river

meanders into the mist

seeking ocean's rest.

Wisconsin River from Ferry Bluff, Sauk County

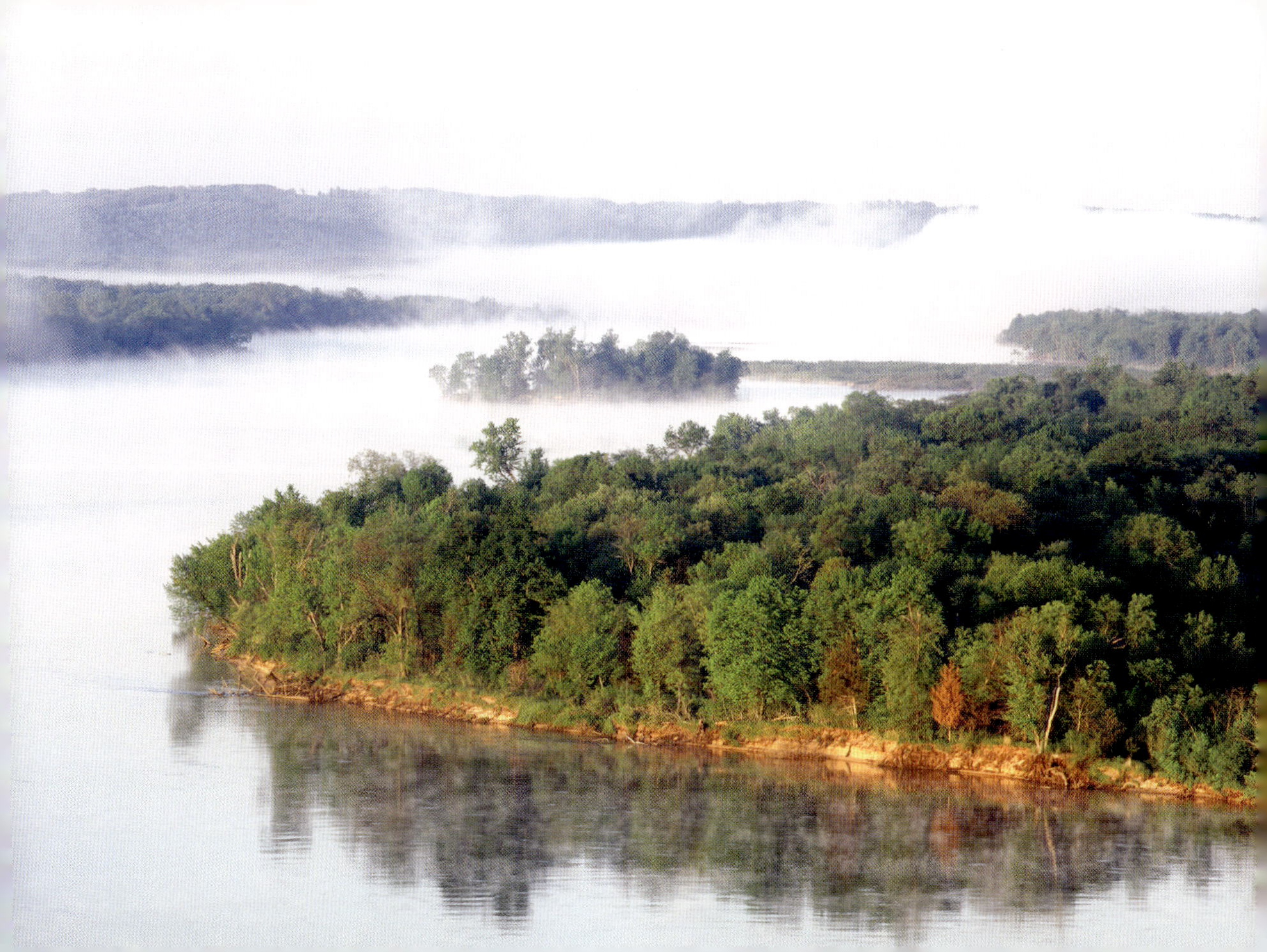

Sailors' warning dawn,

pink with the promise of warmth,

lovely harbor's grace.

Algoma Harbor, Lake Michigan, Algoma

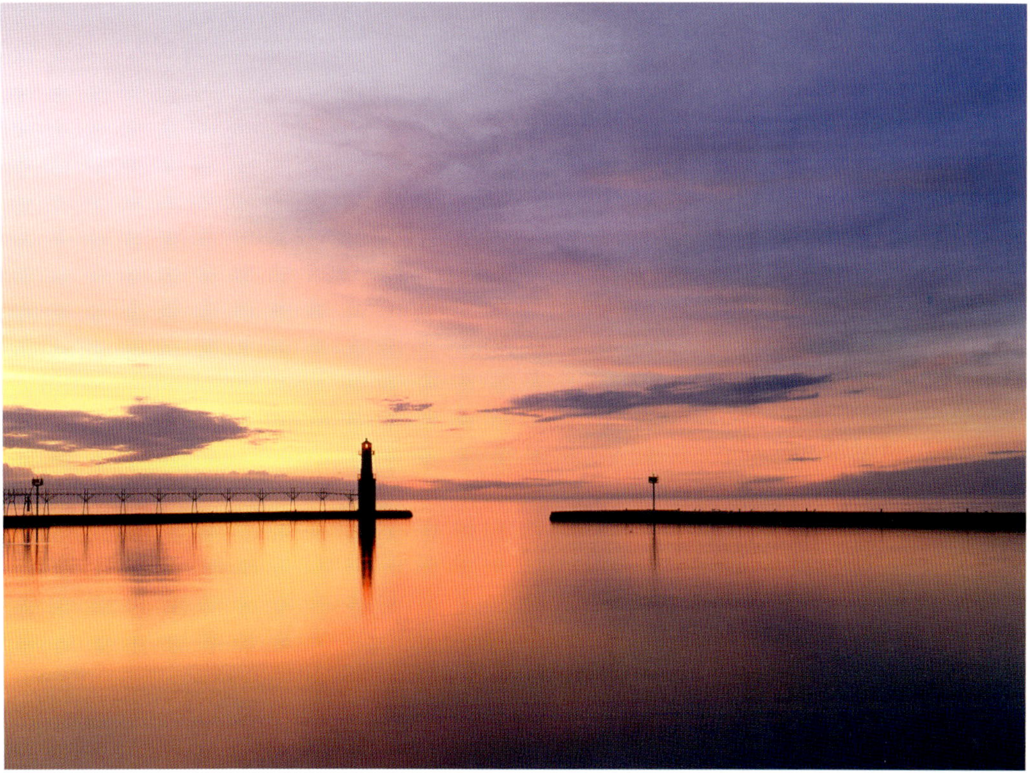

Mississippi dream,

wind and current scratched waters

stretch to salty Gulf.

Sunset over Mississippi River, Alma

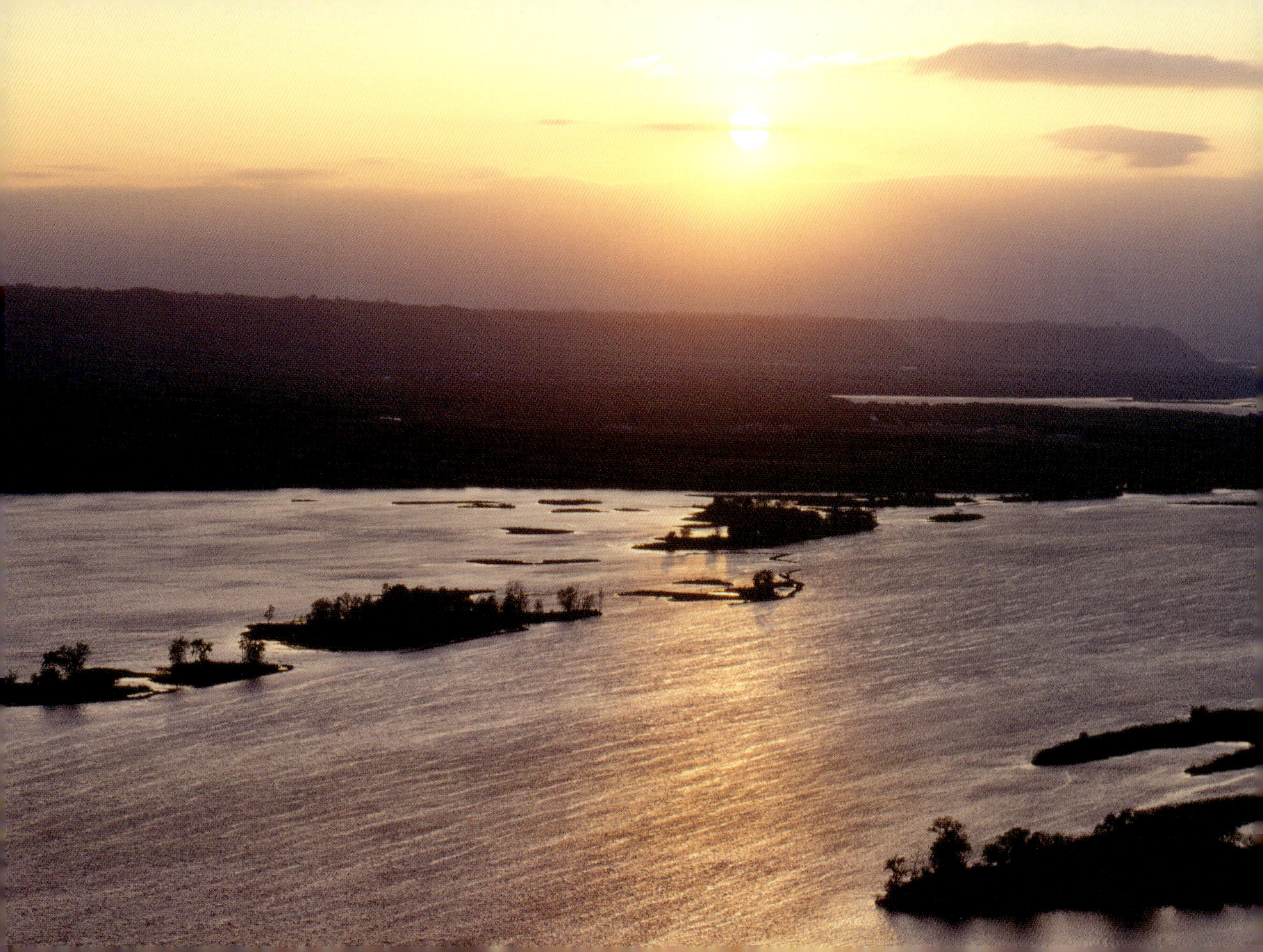

Stark in sunset's light

roots so tangled and exposed,

abandoned, forlorn.

Gile Flowage, Iron County

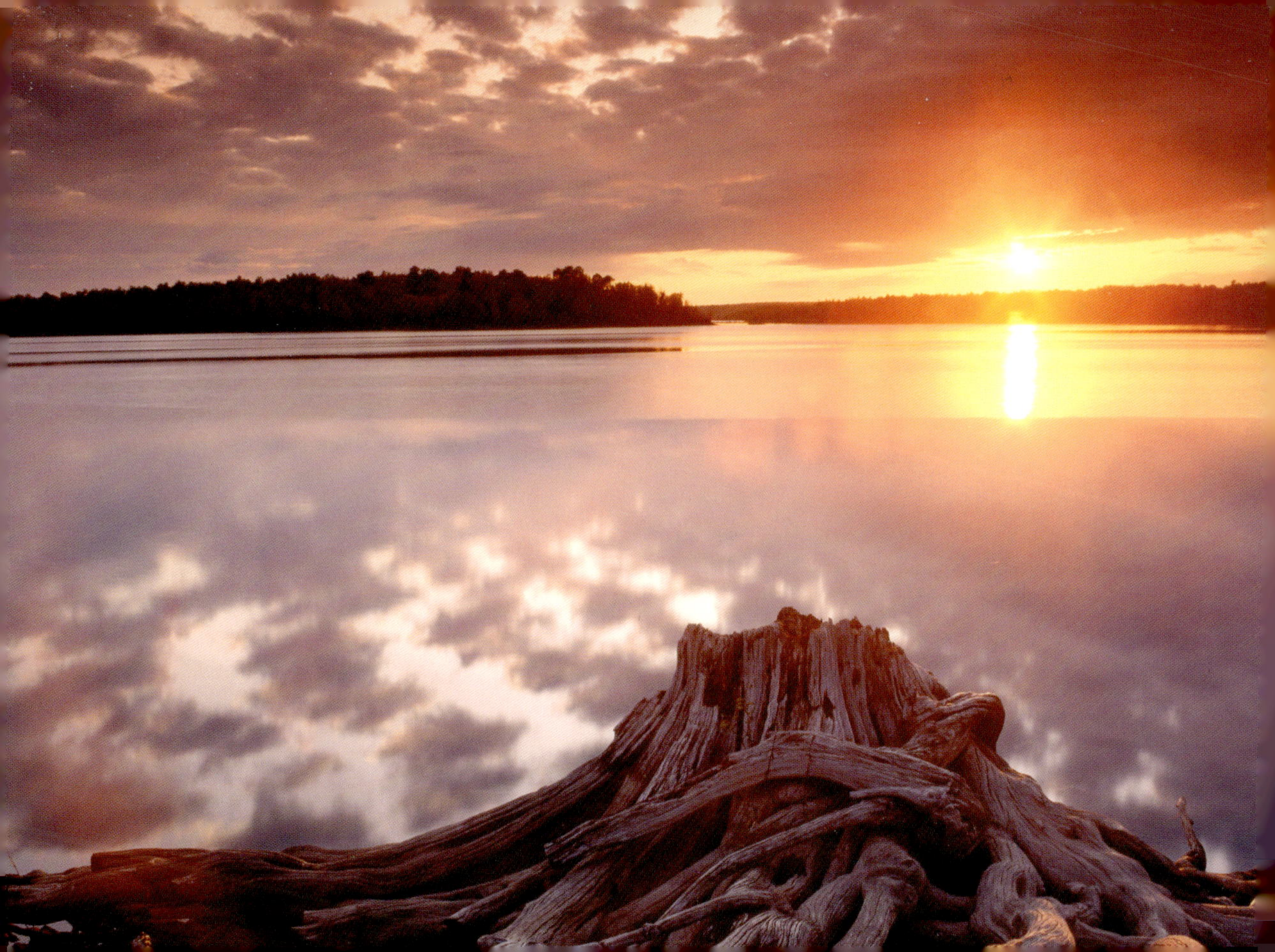

Come, rest your eyes here.

Brilliant crooked symmetry,

delightful repose.

Sunset over Green Bay (near Fish Creek), Door County

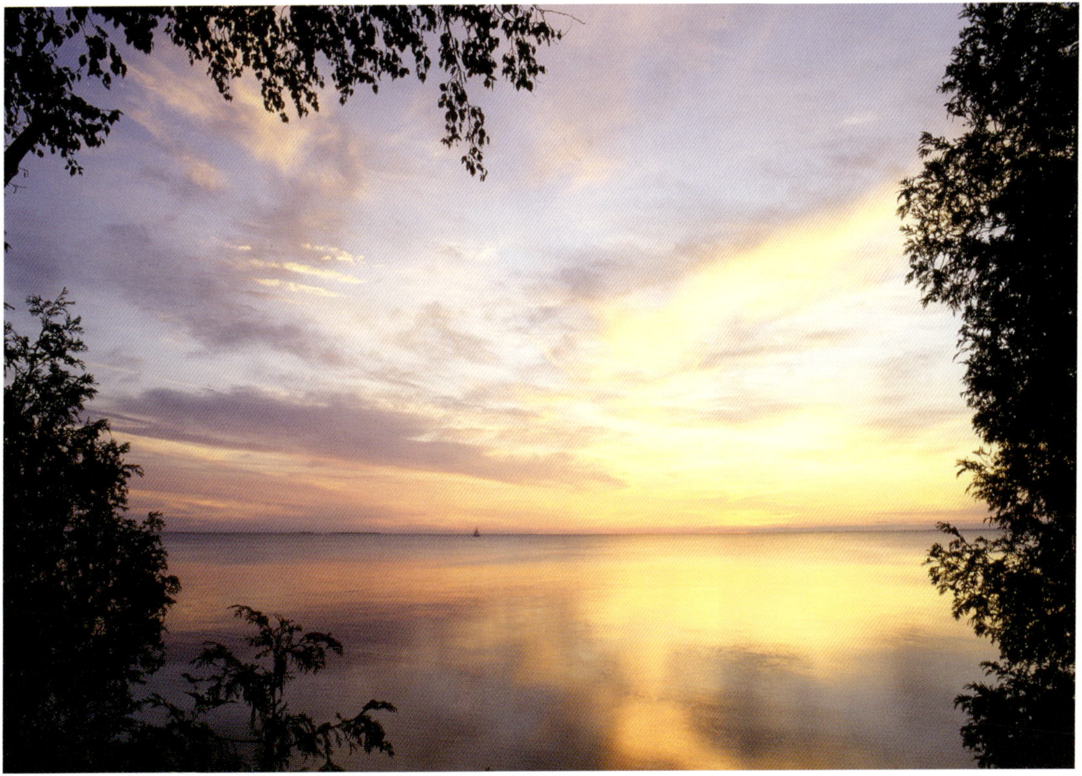

Beauty beyond mind,

misted northern lake sunrise

in all ways pristine.

Carrol Lake, Northern Highlands American Legion State Forest, Oneida County

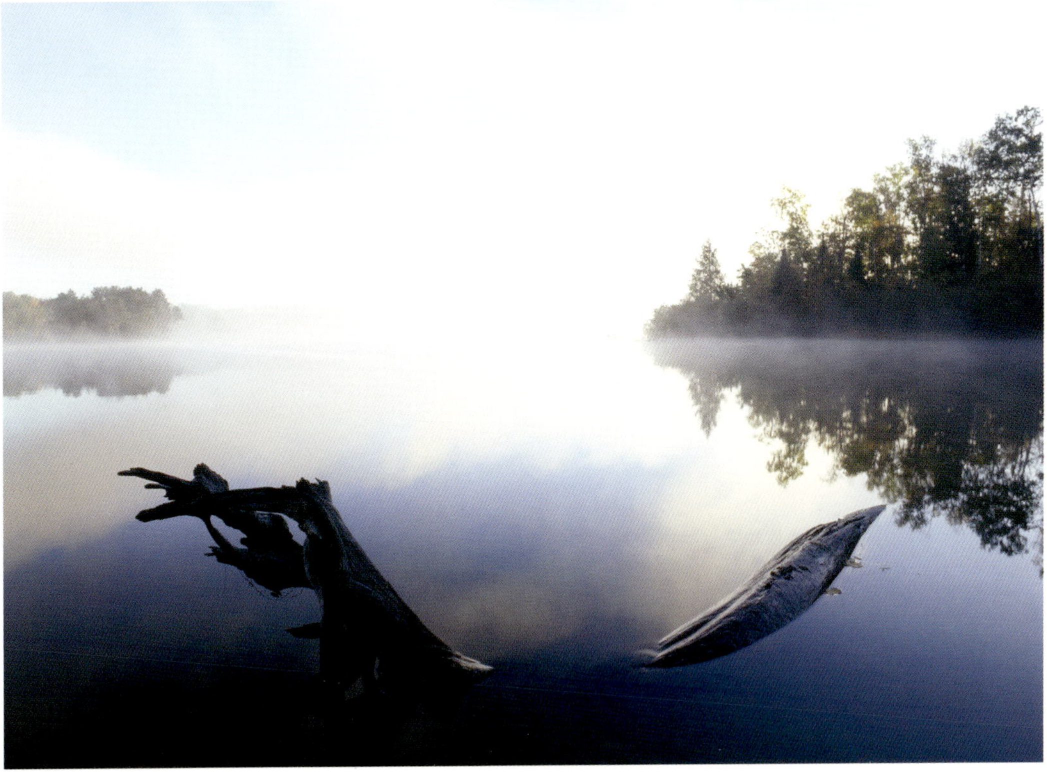

Quiet family scene.

Momma explains to baby,

don't go too far out!

Eagle Bluff and Horseshoe Island, Ephraim, Door County

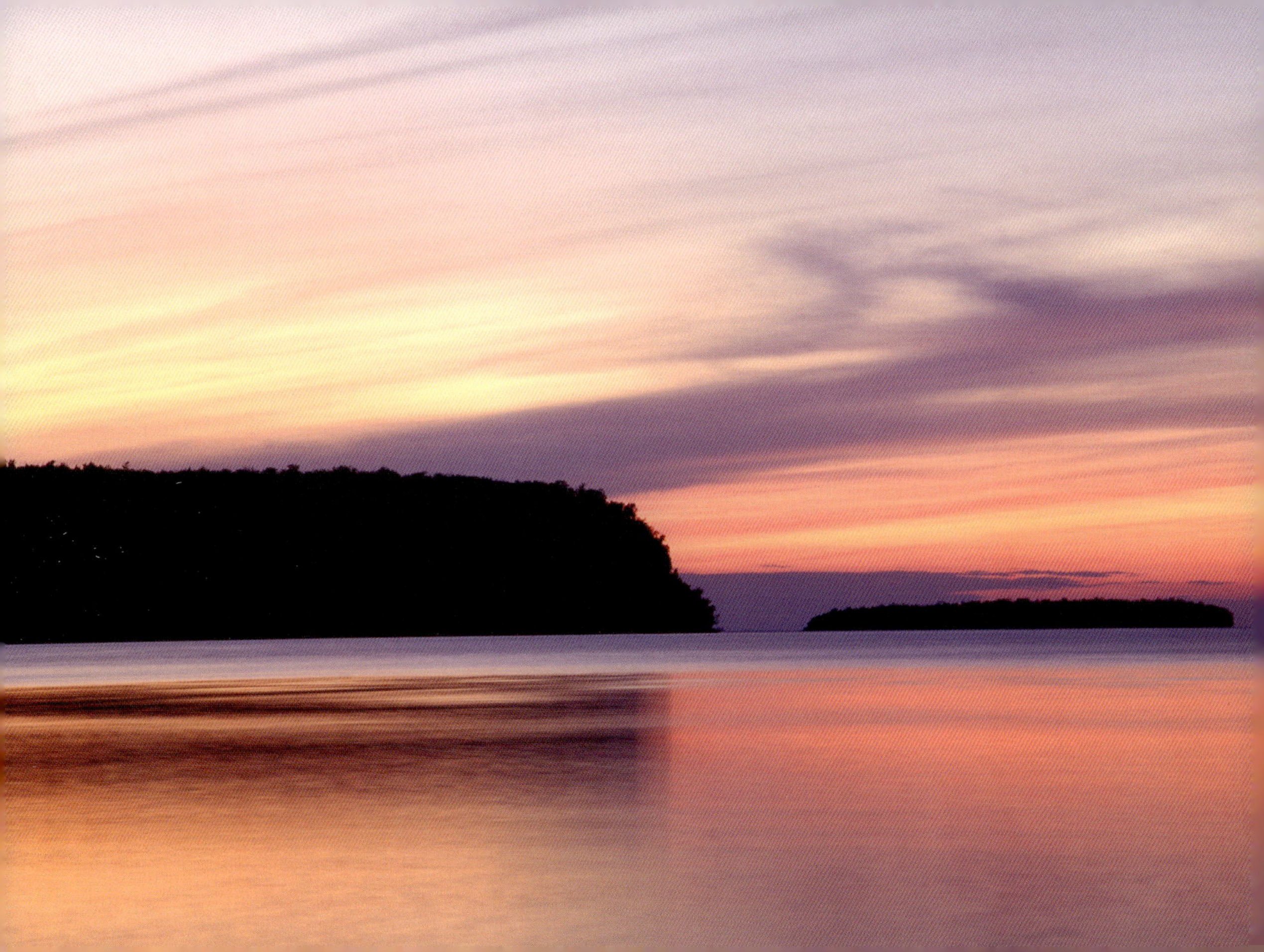

A snug harbor's lights,

cool water in summer's heat

feeling so secure.

Lakeside Park Lighthouse, Lake Winnebago, Fond du Lac

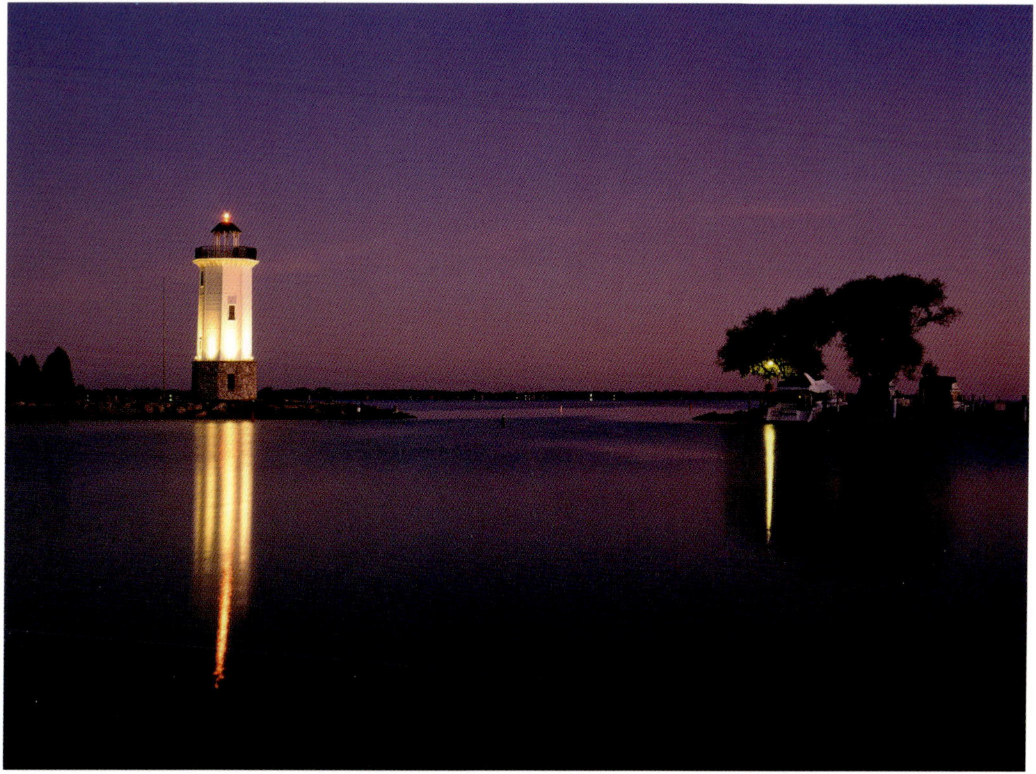

Look! Puddles of ice

so like garden stepping stones

fill this tiny bay.

Sunrise over Lake Michigan, Cave Point County Park, Door County

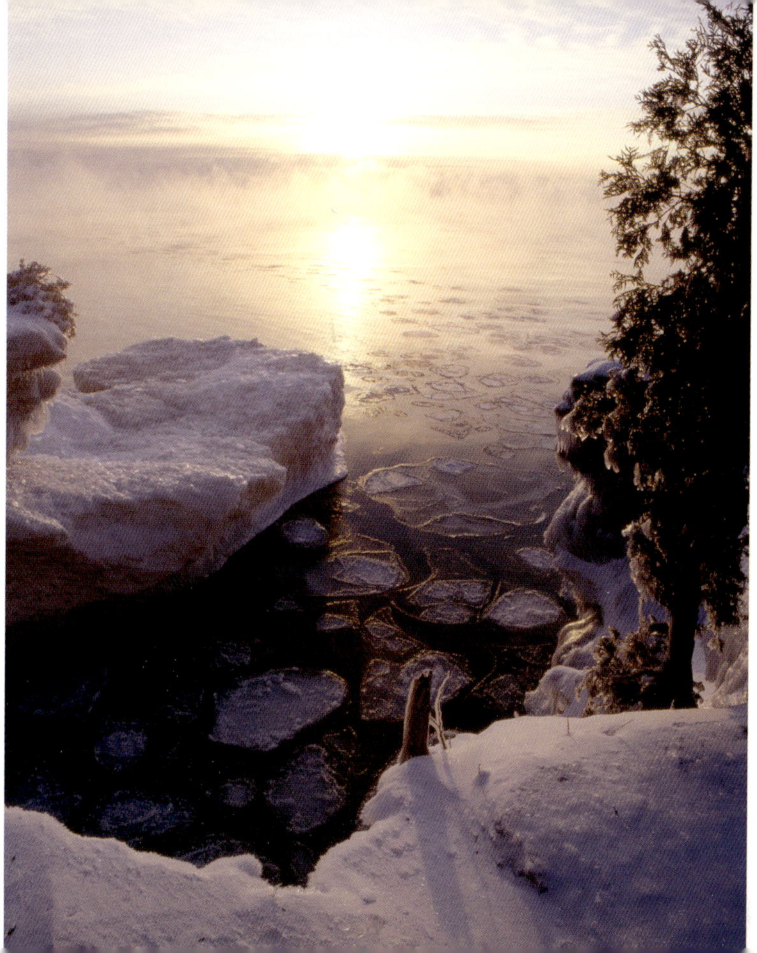

Pointed like ship's prow

this rock defends its cargo

from swift currents deep.

Aspen Leaf on Rock, Lower Cato Falls County Park, Manitowoc River, Manitowoc County

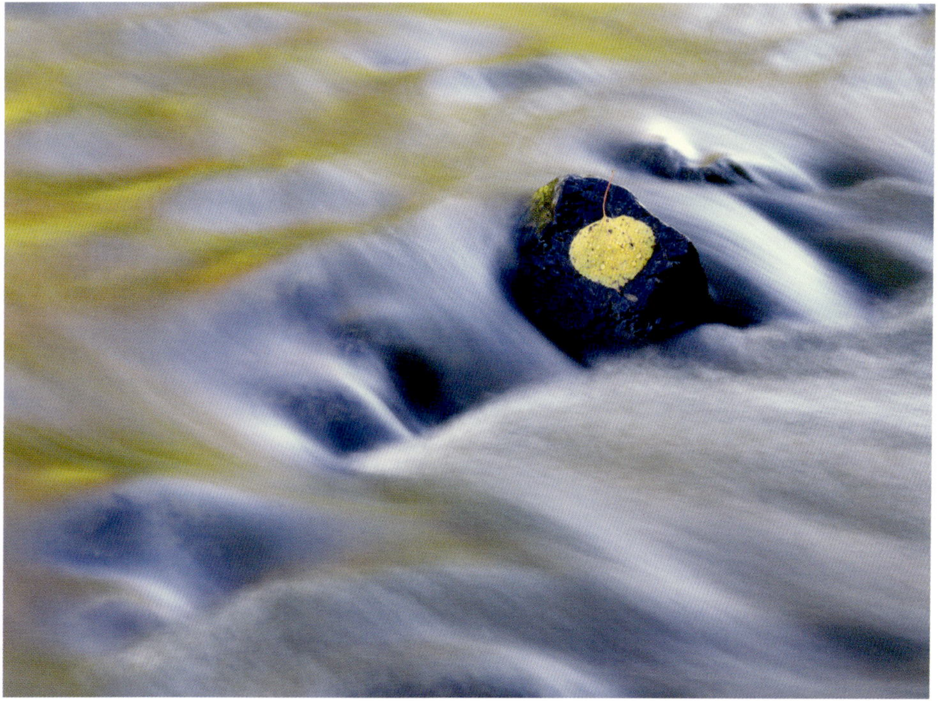

Dancing golden light

nurtures bent cedars each day.

Soon night comes again.

Sunset over Rock Island State Park, Lake Michigan, Door County

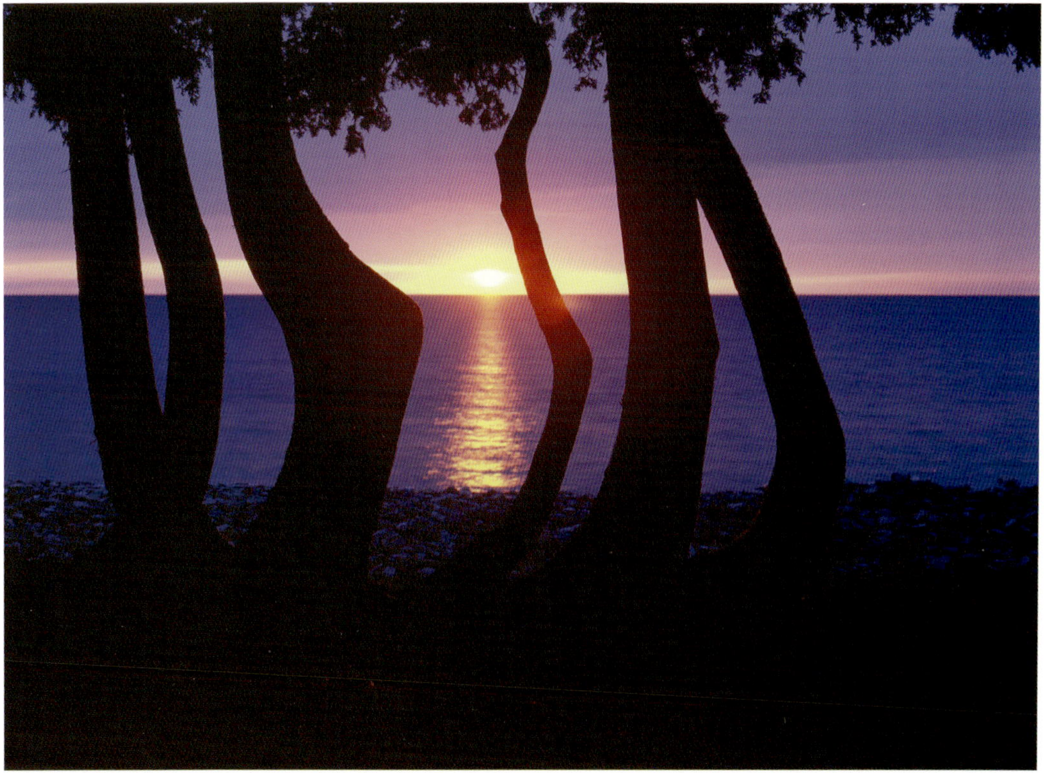

This scene so haunting,

how many have stood right here

gazing as are we?

Carrol Lake, Northern Highlands American Legion State Forest, Oneida County

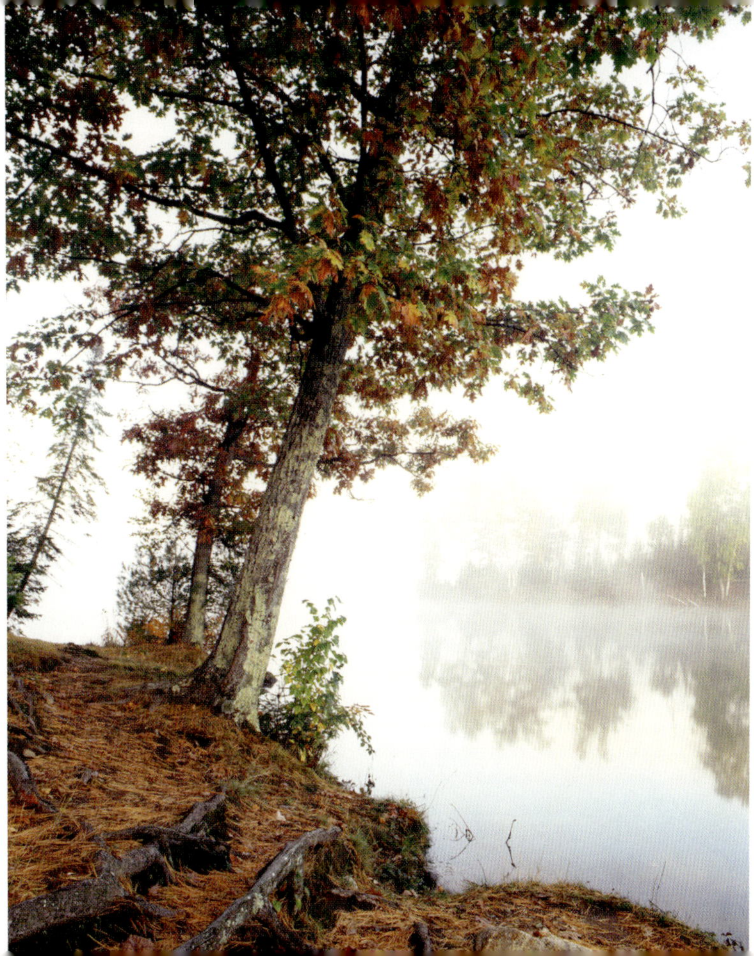

The light bright beneath

these trees now so near drowning,

sun drenched, water quenched.

Black Ash Swamp, Kewaunee County

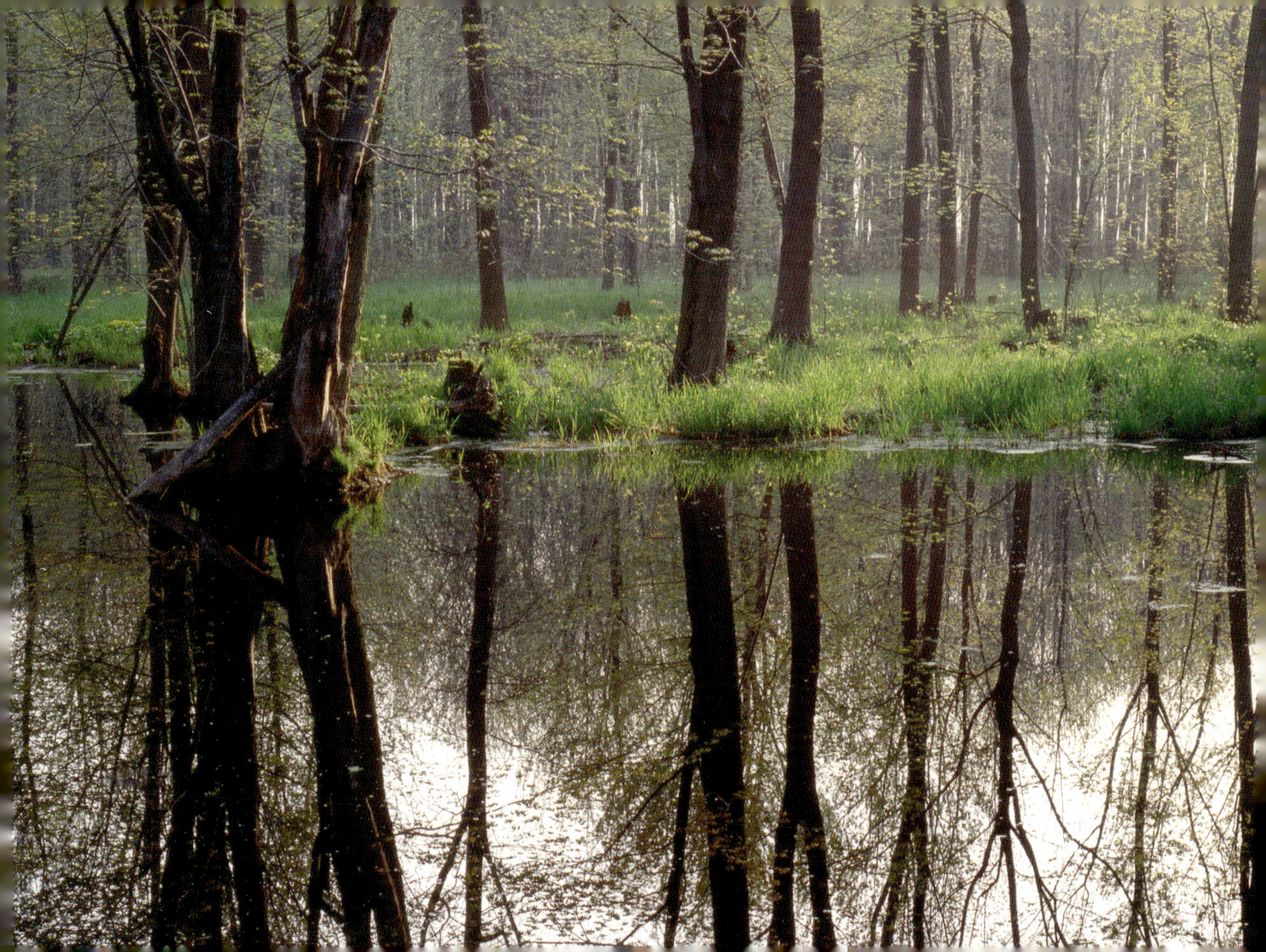

Golden sunset's glow

maple leaf lends perspective,

tiny island home.

Maple Leaf on Rock, Eau Claire River, Dells of the Eau Claire

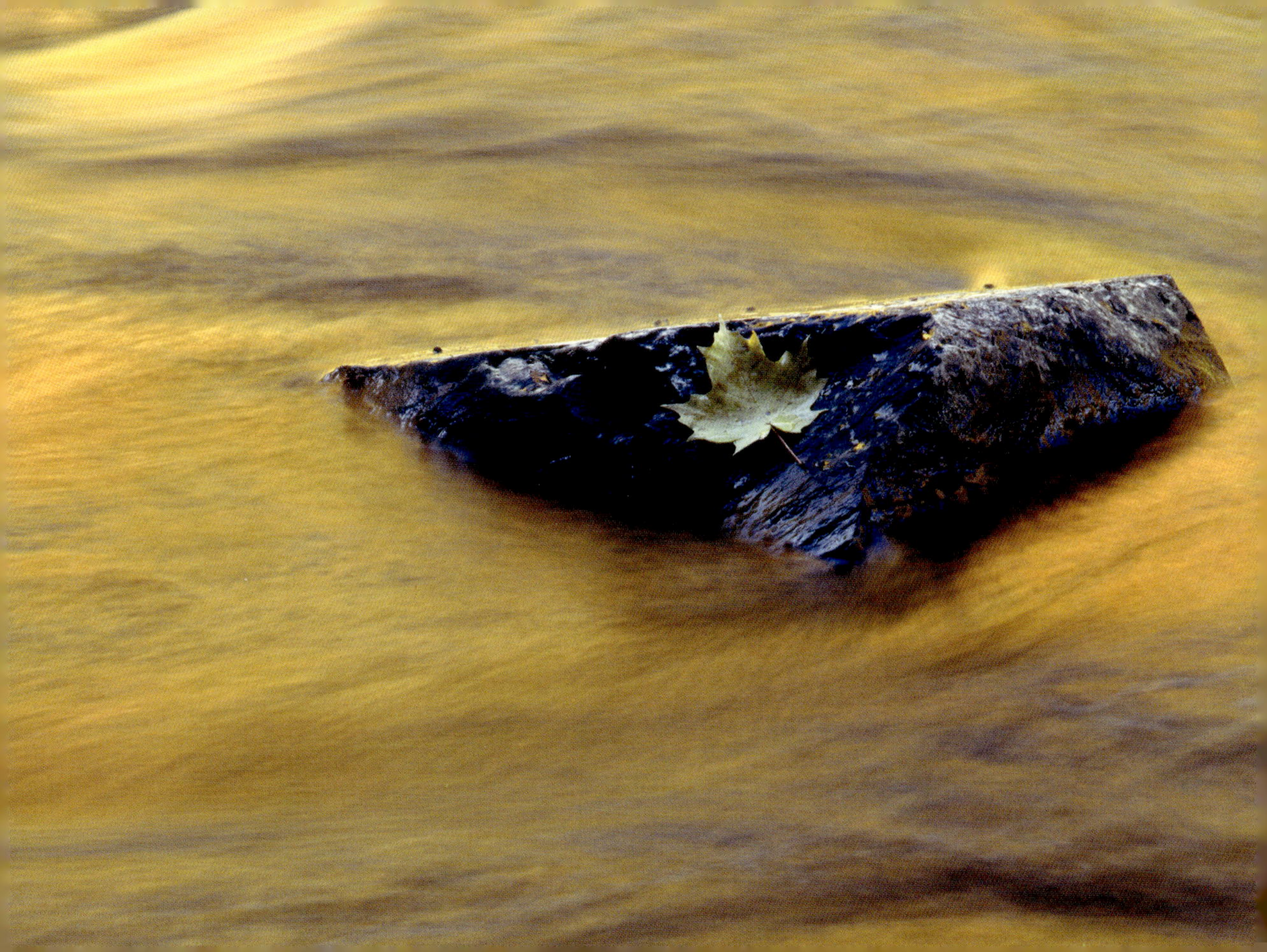

Not red, but golden.

Lake Winnebago's sunset

warms both face and heart.

Lake Winnebago, High Cliff State Park

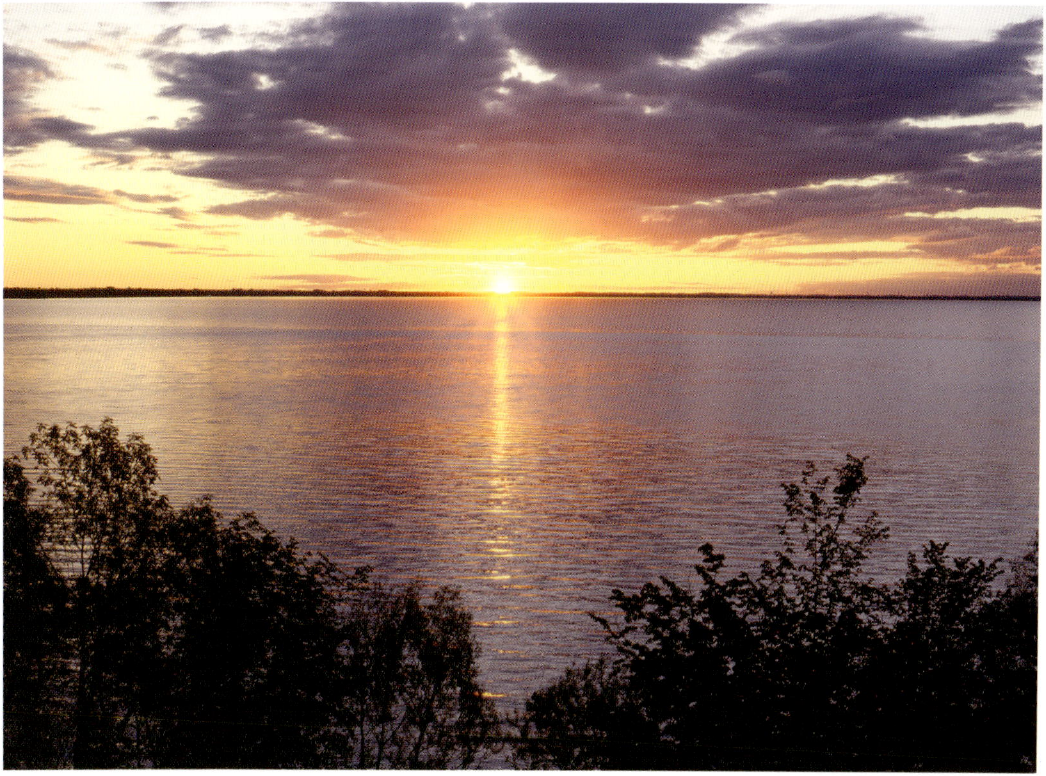

This calm winter shore,

snowy fingers reaching out

welcome a new day.

Winter Dawn, Lake Michigan, Algoma

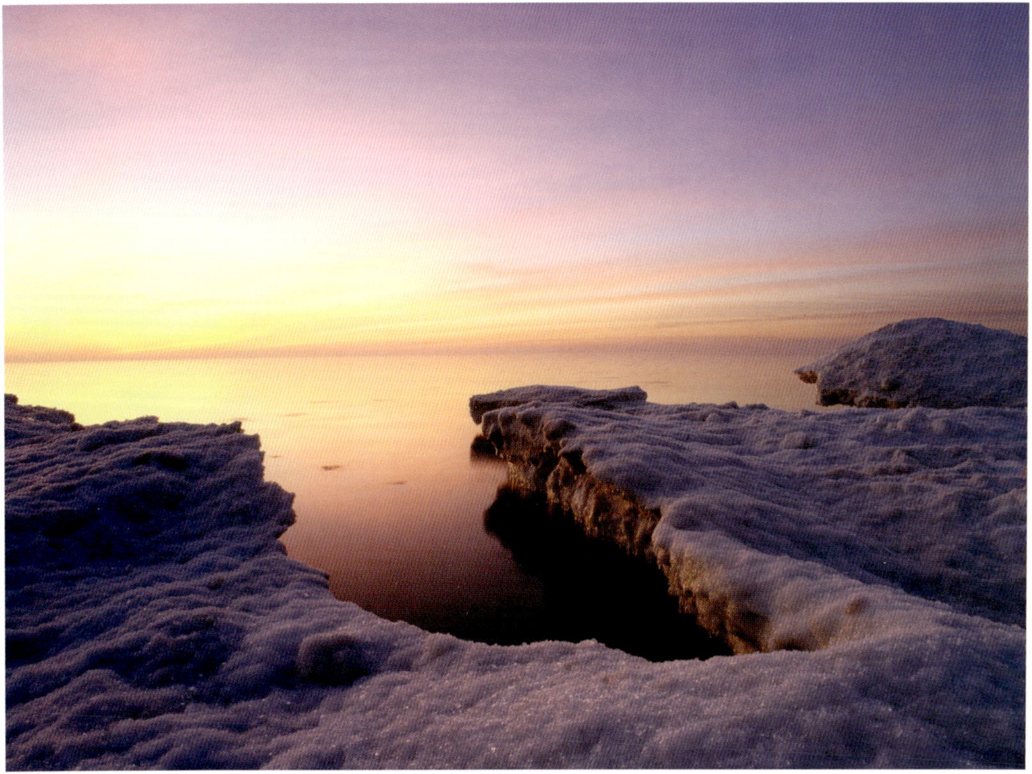

Like a turtle's back

floating in the thick lake mist,

fall colors shine through.

Chain Lake, Oconto County

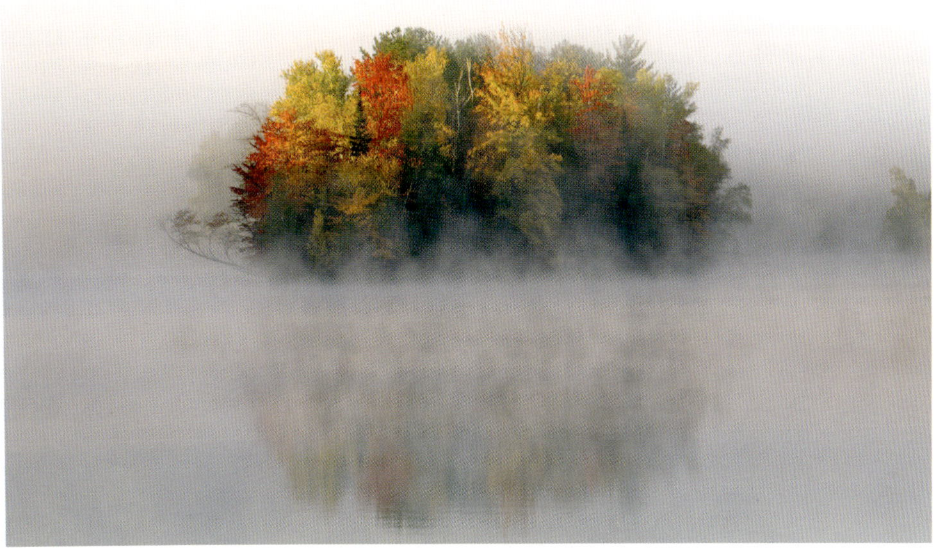

Magical forest,

colors standing steep above

reflect through thin mist.

Turtle Lake, Langlade County

Darryl R. Beers, a self-taught nature/landscape photographer, has spent more than two decades wandering the Great Lakes region creating photographic imagery that captures the essence and the natural beauty of this unique landscape. His photographs have been featured in myriad regional, national, and international publications via books, magazines, calendars, cards, murals, and much more. His fine art photographic prints are found in numerous private collections throughout the United States. For Darryl, photography is the means through which he is able to maintain a spiritual connection to the natural world. His photographs are simply the medium through which his intimate encounters with Nature can be shared with others.

Dr. Raymond Reed Hardy, a retired psychology professor, began exploring the psychological impacts of a wide range of meditation practices in the early 1970s, settling on Zen in 1977. After 22 years of daily zazen, Hardy published his first book, *Zen Master: Practical Zen by an American for Americans* (1999), followed seven years later by *Zen Student: Remember, Live Right Now!* (2006). When asked, "What does meditation, and specifically zazen meditation, have to do with writing haiku?" Hardy replies,

> When one is mindful,
> here now, no past or future,
> haiku fruits ripen.